An Embroidered
Christmas

0 11557 01436 5

An Embroidered
Christmas

Patterns and Instructions for 24 Festive Holiday Stockings, Ornaments, and More

A NeedleKnowledge® Book

Cheryl Fall

STACKPOLE
BOOKS

Published by
STACKPOLE BOOKS
5067 Ritter Road
Mechanicsburg, PA 17055
www.stackpolebooks.com

Printed in the United States of America

10 9 8 7 6 5 4 3 2 1

First edition

Cover design by Caroline Stover

Library of Congress Cataloging-in-Publication Data

Fall, Cheryl.
   An embroidered Christmas : patterns and instructions for 24
festive holiday stockings, ornaments, and more / Cheryl Fall. —
First edition.
      pages cm
   Includes index.
   ISBN 978-0-8117-1436-5
   1. Embroidery—Patterns. 2. Christmas decorations. I. Title.
   TT775.F35 2015
   746.44—dc23
      2015009787

Dedication

This book is dedicated to stitchers around the world who enjoy making beautiful handmade items for the holidays, and who have inspired many of the projects in this book. I hope some of the projects in this book become family heirlooms, passed on and enjoyed by family members and friends for years—and generations—to come.

Contents

Dedication v

Acknowledgments ix

Basic Materials 1

Basic Techniques 7

The Projects 11

Felt Stockings 12

     Paisley Stocking 13

     Mistletoe Stocking 16

Embroidered Nativity Figures 18

Scandinavian Banded Stocking 22

Banded Tree Centerpieces 26

Banded Candle Mat and Napkin Ring 31

Embroidered Ornaments and Wine Bag 35

Naughty or Nice Framed Hoop 39

Heartfelt Christmas Ornaments 42

Noel Banner 44

Christmas Star 48

"We Wish You a Merry Christmas" Framed Sampler 51

Felt Peppermints 54

Stitch Guide 57

Finishing Basics 67

Recommended Resources 77

Terminology 79

Color Conversion and Metric Equivalent Charts 80

Index of Stitches 81

Visual Index 82

Acknowledgments

A hearty "thank you" goes out to my friends at DMC Threads in Kearny, New Jersey. In addition to supplying the bulk of the materials used in this book, they are a great source of inspiration and creative resources. I'd also like to thank the entire Stackpole Books staff for their editorial skills, brilliant design layout, and their help in making this book a reality.

To my grown daughters, Rebecca and Ashley, whose fresh, youthful ideas always inspire me to push the limits with my designs and to "think young;" my husband who never seems to mind the amount of time I spend each day stitching; and my mother, who keeps me motivated.

Basic Materials

Fabrics used in this book

Zigzag edge finish

Fabrics

The projects in this book are made using fabrics that you can readily find at your local needlework shop, hobby and craft chain, or sewing store. Types of fabrics used in the projects include Aida, evenweave, and plain-weave fabrics, as well as wool felt.

Aida fabric is specially woven for cross-stitch, with a weave that contains an even number of vertical and horizontal squares per inch. It is available in a wide variety of counts—the number of squares—per inch. Refer to the project instructions for the count used in each sampler. The fabrics used in this book range from 11- to 16-count and are easy to find at your local needlework or hobby store and through online sources.

Evenweave fabrics have an even number of vertical and horizontal (warp and weft) threads per inch in a plain weave. They are used for the counted thread projects in this book, as well as some of the cross-stitch samplers. When working cross-stitch on evenweave, the pattern will state the number of threads to cross when working the stitches.

Plainweave fabrics are tightly woven evenweave fabrics with threads that are too close together to count. These firmer fabrics are used for the surface-embroidered samplers in this book.

Wool felt is a heavier fabric available at better craft and sewing stores that is made of wool or a wool blend, and is available by the yard or in pre-cut sheets. Pre-cut sizes are 9" x 12" or 12" x 18". I have used the 12" x 18" size for the felt projects in this book, as the 9" x 12" is too small for the stockings, and purchasing by the yard yields a lot of fabric.

All of the woven fabrics should be machine zigzag stitched around the edges to prevent fraying while you're working the stitching.

Threads

Cotton 6-strand embroidery floss has been used for many projects in this book. This floss is made from six individual strands of thread that can be divided into smaller groups of thread. In most cases, two strands are used for cross-stitch and surface embroidery stitches, and a single strand for backstitches or accent stitching.

Specialty threads and pearl cotton have also been used in some of the projects for a thicker line, or to add metallic sparkle or a unique look. Refer to the project instructions for the number of threads to be used while working a project if the thread is dividable.

When shopping for threads online, especially if you are planning on making color substitutions, remember that while the label may indicate the thread is colorfast, it may in fact crock or bleed when laundered. New and revised FDA rules in the U. S. and similar rules abroad have caused changes in dye formulations, making few dyes truly colorfast. While this is meant to keep stitchers safe from harmful chemicals, it also means that an older skein of a certain color may not match a newer skein. While it's easy to blame a manufacturer for this issue, please don't. They go through great pains to ensure the accuracy of their colors, and must conform to the rules regarding chemicals in dyes to stay in business and continue providing you with quality needlework threads. The changes in formulation often do cause a difference in color. To help avoid this issue, be sure to compare the actual color of new and old threads before stitching.

TIP Make sure you have enough of each thread color to complete a project. The older the thread, the greater the chance that the dye formulation used to create the color was different than a new skein.

Needles

There are just three types of needles that are called for when working the projects—tapestry, embroidery, and beading.

Tapestry needles have a blunt tip and a long eye that can accommodate several strands of embroidery floss. The blunt tip allows the needle to pass between the warp and weft fibers in the fabric without catching them, which helps make well-formed stitches.

Embroidery needles have a sharp tip and an eye that can accommodate several strands of floss. The sharp tip allows the needle to pierce the fibers in the fabric, rather than passing next to them. These needles are used for the surface-embroidery samplers or where surface embroidery has been used to add accents to counted-thread and cross-stitch designs.

Beading needles have a long, thin shaft and a small eye that can only accommodate a single strand of thread. These needles are using to attach beads or embellishments to a project.

Refer to the project directions for needle sizes, or use the table below to select the right needle for your project.

Fabric Count	Needle Size	Needle Type
6-count Aida	Size 18	Tapestry (blunt)
8-count Aida	Size 20	Tapestry (blunt)
11-count Aida	Size 22	Tapestry (blunt)
14-count Aida	Size 24	Tapestry (blunt)
16-count Aida	Size 26	Tapestry (blunt)
18-count Aida	Size 28	Tapestry (blunt)

Strand Count	Needle Size	Needle Type
1–2 strands floss	Size 10	Embroidery (sharp)
3–4 strands floss	Size 9 or 8	Embroidery (sharp)
5–6 strands floss	Size 8	Embroidery (sharp)
Size 5 Pearl Cotton	Size 6	Embroidery (sharp)
Size 8 Pearl Cotton	Size 8	Embroidery (sharp)
Size 12 Pearl Cotton	Size 10	Embroidery (sharp)

TIP Blunt tapestry needles pass through the space between two threads in an evenweave fabric or between the squares in Aida fabric, while sharp embroidery needles pierce the fibers in plainweave embroidery fabrics.

Scissors, Hoops, and Notions

In addition to the needles, threads, and fabrics, there are other items you will need to work the projects in this book. These are notions that are a basic part of any embroidery or sewing workbag and include scissors in several sizes (large shears for cutting fabric and small embroidery scissors for cutting thread), embroidery hoops in several sizes and shapes to hold the fabric taut while working the stitching, a measuring tape or ruler, and pens or pencils for marking the cloth or transferring a design to your fabric.

Other handy items to keep in your bag include thimbles, tweezers, a nail file in case of burrs, thread conditioner for use with unruly threads, a magnetic needle keeper, plastic or cardboard bobbins for wrapping leftover embroidery threads for safekeeping, and a stitch guide.

TIP Completely separate all strands of embroidery floss and regroup them before using them. This will result in a smoother finished stitch and help prevent tangling.

Basic Techniques

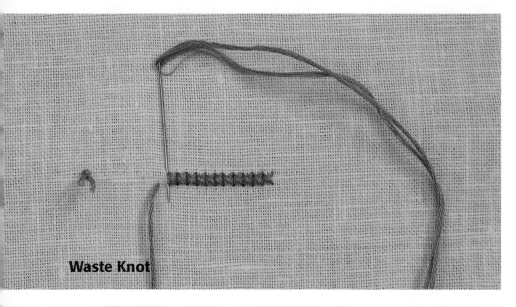

Waste Knot

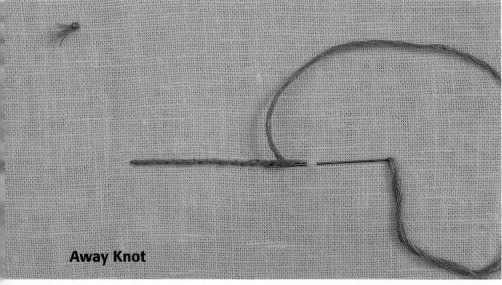

Away Knot

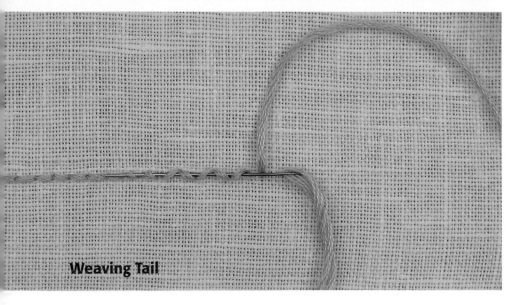

Weaving Tail

Starting and Ending Your Thread

The first rule of "embroiderydom" is: No knots—not ever—unless they are an integral part of the design. Permanent knots are not only unnecessary, but they can come undone after the project is used or laundered, causing stitch loss. They also cause bumps and ugly tails on the back side of the work.

You should always start and end with a tail of thread that passes underneath the thread on the back side of the work. The use of two temporary knots will aid you in this purpose.

A *waste knot* can be made when working cross-stitch or counted-thread projects. To use a waste knot, place your knot so that it will be directly in the line of stitching. Once you have overstitched the tail of the thread and it is secured under the stitching, clip the knot and trim the tail.

An *away knot* is a temporary knot that is made a few inches from where your stitching is set to begin, and is handy for surface embroidery projects. After you have completed stitching the area, the knot is clipped from the piece, the resulting tail threaded through the eye of the needle, and the tail woven through the stitching on the back side of the work.

Keeping your work knot-free with these techniques is easy, and will not only keep the back of your work tidy, but will also keep your heirlooms from unraveling in the years to come.

Determining and Changing Thread Count

All of the designs in this book tell you what fabric was used to make the sample shown in the photograph. Using the fabric given in the directions will ensure that the patterns for cutting will fit the embroidered area. If you decide to change the fabric, be aware that the item will be either larger or smaller than the original design. For example, if you decide to use 18-count Aida in the Scandinavian Banded Stocking instead of 11-count, your finished stocking will be much smaller than the 12" x 18" stocking shown in the sample image.

However, if you wish to use a piece of fabric that you already have in your stash but are unsure of the finished size of the piece, here's the simple math:

1. Determine the number of stitches along the top (horizontal) edge and one side (vertical) edge of the pattern. This is done by counting the number of squares in the pattern grid. To make things easier, there are 10 small squares for each larger square in the grid.
2. Divide the numbers from step 1 by the thread count. In this example I am using 60 vertical stitches and 80 horizontal stitches:
   - 6-count Aida equals a finished size of 10" x 13.33"
   - 8-count Aida equals a finished size of 7.5" x 10"
   - 11-count Aida equals a finished size of 5.45" x 7.27"
   - 14-count Aida equals a finished size of 4.28" x 5.71"
   - 16-count Aida equals a finished size of 3.75" x 5"

Marking Your Fabric

Fold the fabric into quarters and mark the vertical and horizontal centers. Using a washable, water-soluble marking pen or pencil (not a permanent pen or heat transfer pen), draw a line along a single fiber of fabric to mark the centers. Or, using a single strand of 6-strand floss, mark the centers using running stitch along the ditch between two strands of warp and weft threads in the fabric. You will use these lines as a guide when you transfer the pattern.

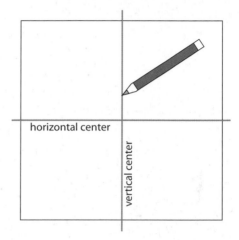

horizontal center

vertical center

There are a few different ways to transfer patterns. Try them each to see which you prefer. If you choose to use heat transfer pencils, make sure they have sharp points so that you will transfer a clean line that can easily be covered with thread as you work the embroidery. Also note that patterns must be transferred in reverse when using transfer pencils, as the process creates a mirror image of the design.

Reversed pattern traced on lightweight paper

Remove paper pattern after heat transfer to fabric

Follow the directions indicated on the pencil packaging for best results, as the wax-based inks can vary among brands.

When transferring designs to heavy fabric, such as the red felt Paisley Stocking or the green felt Mistletoe Stocking, you can also use Glad® Press'n Seal®. It's a terrific way to transfer an embroidery design to other types of thick fabrics, too, such as velvet or wool. To transfer a design using this method, cut a piece of Press'n Seal to fit the embroidery pattern. Lay the wrap over the paper pattern carefully to avoid wrinkles or bubbles. Using a fine-line permanent pen, trace the pattern directly onto the top of the wrap. For larger images, use multiple lengths of wrap.

After the design has been traced, carefully adhere the wrap to the front side of the embroidery fabric, and press in place. Work the design through both the wrap and the fabric.

Once the embroidery has been finished, carefully peel away the wrap, using tweezers to remove the bits stuck under the stitching or in small, tight areas. There are no markings to remove later by laundering, making this method ideal for fabrics that can't be washed in water.

Reading a Cross-Stitch or Counted-Thread Chart— Where to Begin

It's easiest to follow a pattern for a counted cross-stitch or counted-thread project by working from the center outward. You can locate the center of the pattern by finding the arrows along the outside edge of the grid and noting where they intersect.

The Projects

Felt Stockings

PAISLEY STOCKING

Make a set of felt stockings. The first design is a Paisley Stocking that resembles a bandana print and is worked in a classic, red wool felt. The stocking can easily be worked in green as a companion, or invert the colors by stitching in green or red thread on white felt. You could have a matched set of stockings by simply changing the color placement. Because of its bandana look, you could also stitch it on blue or brown felt for a Western look.

Materials Needed

- Two 12" x 18" pieces of red wool felt
- Glad® Press'n Seal®
- Fine-point permanent marker
- Size 5 Pearl Cotton in white (DMC B5200)
- DMC Light Effects Precious Metal Effects Floss, color E3821
- Size 6/0 E beads in gold
- Size 6 embroidery needle
- Beading needle

Directions

1. Referring to the directions in the Basic Techniques chapter (pages 9–10), trace the embroidery design for the full stocking onto a piece of Glad® Press'n Seal® using a fine-point waterproof marker. Carefully adhere the design to the front side of one of the pieces of red felt, keeping the wrap smooth and free from wrinkles or bubbles.

2. Stitching through the wrap and the felt, embroider the large paisley shapes in coral stitch using the size 5 pearl cotton and a size 6 embroidery (sharp) needle. Work the dotted lines in French knots using the same thread.

3. Embroider the dashed lines in the large paisley shapes using two strands of the gold, 6-strand Light Effects floss in backstitch. To prevent tangling when using this metallic thread, work in shorter lengths than you would for a cotton thread—10 to 12 inches is a good length.

4. Using the size 5 pearl cotton, embroider the smaller paisley shapes in backstitch and the little blossoms in lazy daisy.

5. After the embroidery has been completed, *carefully remove* the wrap. Use small tweezers to pull the bits that are stuck in tight corners or under the stitches. Work in small sections. Do not tug as this could warp the felt.

6. Once the wrap has been removed, stitch a gold bead to the center of each blossom using a beading needle.

7. Cut the stocking shape from the embroidered section and from the second piece of felt (the backing) and finish the stocking as shown on pages 70–72.

Full Stocking after Joining Sections

Full-Size Paisley Stocking Bottom

Full-Size Paisley Stocking Top

MISTLETOE STOCKING

The second felt stocking is the Mistletoe Stocking. It is made in a similar manner to the Paisley Stocking, utilizing Glad® Press'n Seal® to help facilitate embroidering on heavy wool felt without leaving marks behind. The simple repeating pattern can be used to make a stocking in nearly any size by adding to the rows.

Materials Needed

- Two 12" x18" pieces of green wool felt
- Glad® Press'n Seal®
- Fine-point permanent marker
- Size 5 Pearl Cotton in white (DMC B5200)
- DMC Light Effects Precious Metal Effects Floss, color E3821
- Size 6/0 E beads in gold
- Size 6 embroidery needle
- Beading needle

Directions

1. Referring to the directions in the Basic Techniques chapter (pages 9–10), trace the embroidery design for the full stocking onto a piece of Glad® Press'n Seal® using a fine-point waterproof marker. To do this, trace the outline of the full-size Paisley Stocking pattern on pages 14–15, then fill in with the full-size Mistletoe design from page 17, as shown to the right. Carefully adhere the design to the front side of one of the pieces of green felt, keeping the wrap smooth and free from wrinkles or bubbles.

2. Stitching through the wrap and the felt, embroider the leaf repeats using size 5 pearl cotton and a size 6 embroidery (sharp) needle.

3. Embroider the dashed lines between the leaf rows using two strands of the gold, 6-strand Light Effects floss in backstitch. To prevent tangling when using this metallic thread, work in shorter lengths than you would for a cotton thread—10 to 12 inches is a good length.

4. After the embroidery has been completed, *carefully remove* the wrap. Use small tweezers to pull the bits that are stuck in tight corners or under the stitches. Work in small sections. Do not tug as this could warp the felt.

5. Once the wrap has been removed, stitch two gold beads to each branch on the leaf units using a beading needle.

6. Cut the stocking shape from the embroidered section and from the second piece of felt (the backing) and finish the stocking as shown on pages 70–72.

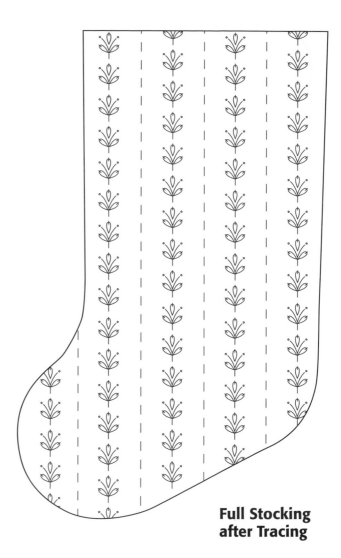

Full Stocking after Tracing

Full-Size Mistletoe Pattern

Embroidered Nativity Figures

This embroidered set featuring the Holy Family is worked in bright, cheerful colors and is perfect for use in a home with kids or boisterous pets, where a breakable nativity isn't an option. In fact, this set is guaranteed to be unbreakable!

I haven't given color names in the materials list, as it's time for you to get creative. Select the hair colors and skin colors for the figures, as well as for their clothing. The set can be easily customized and easily stitched using materials you have on hand. It's a perfect way to use up odds and ends of embroidery floss—anything goes!

Materials Needed

- DMC 6-strand embroidery floss in an assortment of colors, including flesh tones and hair-color tones, along with an assortment of ten to twelve bright colors of floss for the clothing
- One 16" x 20" piece of 32-count linen fabric in white
- Size 10 embroidery needle
- White sewing thread
- Lightweight iron-on interfacing
- Polyester fiberfill or your favorite stuffing material

18

Directions

1. Cut the linen into two 16" x 10" pieces. Set one piece aside to be used as the backing fabric for the figures. Trace the figures onto the linen, spacing them 4 inches apart.

2. Embroider the designs using two strands of the 6-strand floss, mixing the colors in each figure. Use a variety of stitches to work the designs. For example, while backstitch can be used to outline the solid lines for the faces and hands, use stem stitch to work a bolder line in the clothing.

3. The small leaf-shaped areas can be worked in detached chain stitch, while other areas lend themselves perfectly to fern and feather stitching. To see how I worked the figures, take a close look at the photos. Hint: I used French knots with tails to work the halos.

4. After completing the embroidery, trim down the figures to within $1/2$ inch of their outline (see illustration below). Wash the figures to remove the markings by gently swishing them in a bowl of soapy water, then rinsing and drying flat on a towel. Press them while still damp.

5. Cut a piece of the iron-on interfacing for each piece, using the cut-out figures as a pattern. Using a press cloth over the embroidery to protect it from the iron, press the interfacing to the wrong side of the figures.

6. The figures can now be finished as ornaments, using the directions on pages 74–75. They can be hung on the tree, or you can stand them up on a cupboard or the mantel to display.

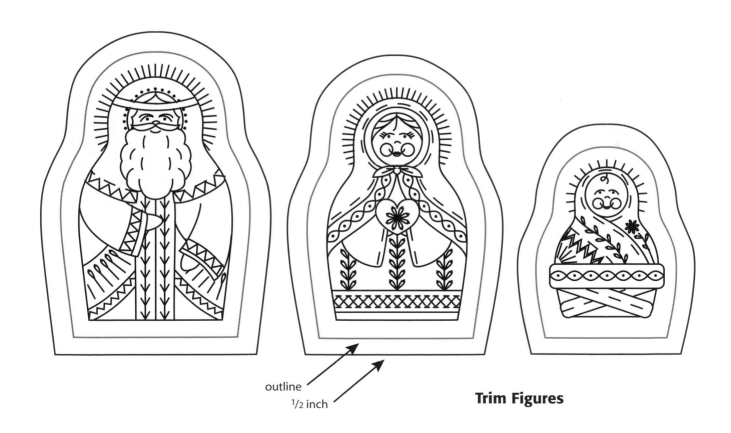

outline

$1/2$ inch

Trim Figures

Joseph (Full Size)

Jesus (Full Size)

Mary (Full Size)

Scandinavian Banded Stocking

I'm madly in love with this stocking. While it looks very involved and complicated, it's created by stitching multiple bands and rows on Aida fabric with large squares, which makes the work of stitching fly by. The bands are very versatile as well, as you'll see in the next two projects.

I'll be stitching one of these in the opposite colorway—in white thread on red Aida—to make a matched set. They'll look fabulous hanging on my mantle this holiday season!

Materials Needed

- 11-count Aida, 18" x 24"
- Machine sewing thread in the same color as the Aida
- DMC 6-strand embroidery floss in color #115 Variegated Red
- 12" x 18" piece of red wool felt for the backing
- Size 11/0 red glass seed beads
- Size 22 or 24 tapestry needle
- Beading needle

Directions

1. Because of its size, the stocking pattern has been given in two sections—a top section and a bottom section. I recommend that you make a copy of each section and tape the patterns together at the center, where indicated by the arrows on the patterns. This will make it easier to keep track of the rows.

2. To work the design, fold the piece of Aida in half to mark the center. Start stitching the stocking at the center, working the cross-stitches using two strands of the 6-strand floss and the backstitch areas using a single strand of floss.

3. Attach a seed bead to each location indicated by a small dot, using the beading needle and a single strand of floss.

4. After you have worked the design, mark the stocking outline on the fabric using a water-soluble marking pen. Trim the stocking shape $1/2$ inch from the marked lines and finish the stocking, referring to the instructions on pages 70–72. This stocking and the two felt stockings are all finished in the same manner and are the same size.

Full Stocking

■ cross-stitch
\ backstitch
● seed bead

Full-Size Stocking Top

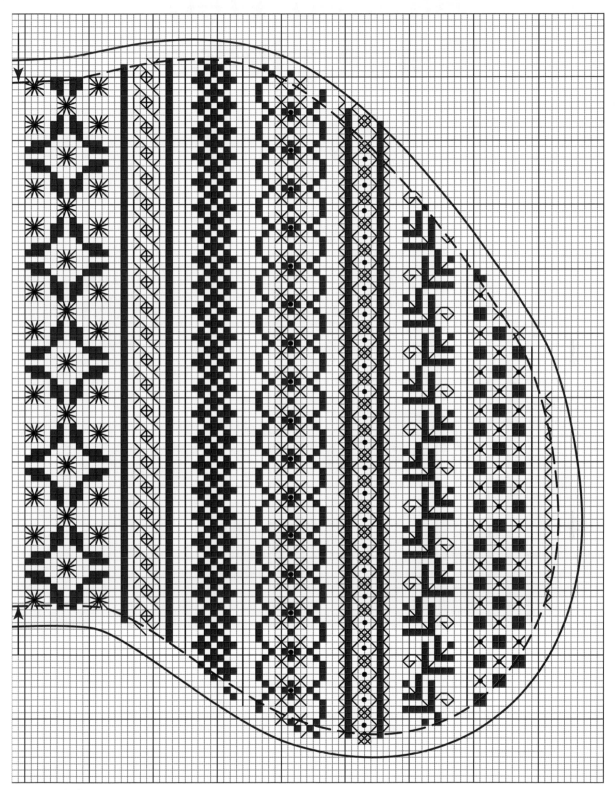

■ cross-stitch
╲ backstitch
● seed bead

Full-Size Stocking Bottom

Banded Tree Centerpieces

Simple bands of cross-stitch and backstitch were used to stitch this forest of trees. I used 11-count Aida to make the largest trees possible, but you can easily substitute a larger count to make smaller trees to add to your forest, giving you a range of sizes. Or, simply add or remove bands from the trees to make other sizes.

Materials Needed

- 11-count Aida, 8" x 10" for the small tree, 11" x 13" for the medium tree, and 12" x 14" for the large tree
- Machine sewing thread in the same color as the Aida
- DMC 6-strand embroidery floss in color #115 Variegated Red
- Red or white fabric for backing
- Trim for edging the trees (optional)
- Size 11/0 red glass seed beads
- Size 22 or 24 tapestry needle
- Beading needle
- Polyester fiberfill stuffing
- Three 1¹/₂" x 2¹/₈" unfinished wooden spools
- Three ³/₈" unfinished wooden dowels, 8", 10", and 12" in length
- Red acrylic craft paint to match the red used in the stitching
- Paintbrush
- Clear-drying glue

Directions

1. Fold each piece of Aida cloth into quarters to locate the center. Stitch each of the trees from the center outward, working the cross-stitch areas using two strands of the 6-strand floss, and the backstitch areas using a single strand. Stitch beads in place wherever you see a small dot, using the beading needle and a single strand of floss.

2. When the stitching has been completed, mark the outline of each tree, as indicated on the patterns, on both the Aida and backing fabric. Cut out the tree shapes 1/2 inch from the marked lines.

3. Place each tree, right side down, on the backing fabric. Machine stitch around each tree using a 1/2-inch seam allowance, leaving a 2-inch opening at the bottom of each tree. Clip the corners and points close to—but not through—the stitching line and turn the tree shapes right side out. Lightly stuff with fiberfill.

4. To make the tree bases, glue a dowel inside the center hole of each wooden spool and let the glue dry. Paint the bases with two coats of acrylic craft paint and let the paint dry overnight.

5. Insert a base into the bottom opening of each tree. Stitch the openings at the bases of the trees closed by hand, making sure you keep the dowel centered. Place a dab of glue at the base of each tree where it meets the dowel. Attach the trim as described on pages 74–75 to complete the trees.

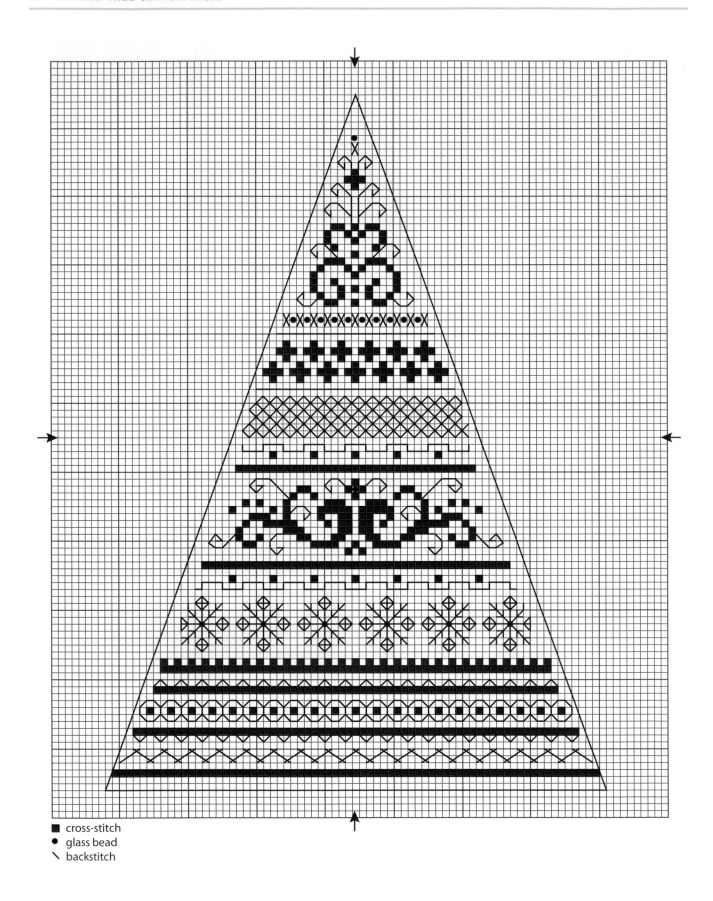

Tree 1 (Full Size)

■ cross-stitch
● glass bead
＼ backstitch

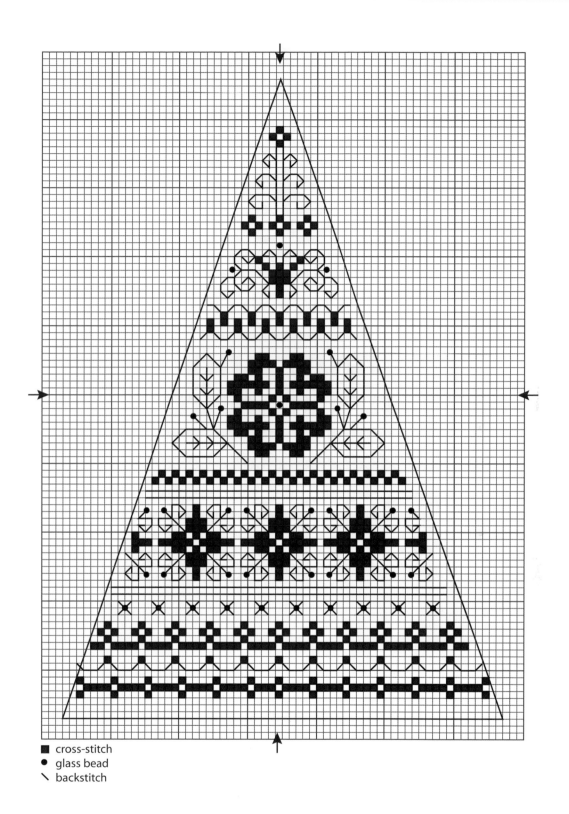

■ cross-stitch
● glass bead
╲ backstitch

Tree 2 (Full Size)

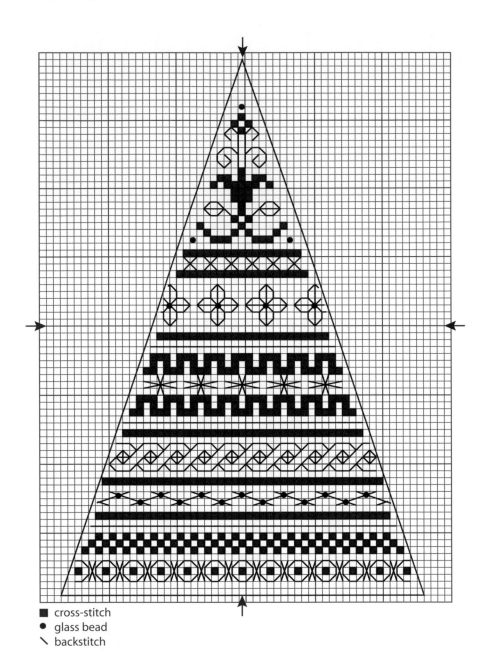

■ cross-stitch
● glass bead
╲ backstitch

Tree 3 (Full Size)

Banded Candle Mat
and Napkin Ring

I just couldn't resist showing you how the bands in the trees and the stocking can be used or adapted to make matching accessories. The stripes are so versatile that I know we can come up with even more ideas! Meanwhile, here are two that will inspire you to use the bands and borders for other projects.

Materials Needed

- 11-count Aida scraps
- Scraps of red wool felt
- Machine sewing thread in the same color as the Aida
- DMC 6-strand embroidery floss in color #115 Variegated Red
- Size 22 or 24 tapestry needle

CANDLE MAT

Directions

1. For the mat, cut a 12" x 12" square of Aida. Fold the cloth into quarters and mark the center. Stitch the design in the center of the square using two strands of the floss for the cross-stitch and a single strand of the floss for the backstitched lines.

2. After you have completed the stitching, trim down the excess Aida so that there are fourteen open, unstitched squares around all four sides of the fabric. Remove the threads in the squares eight squares in from the outside edge of the border, forming a channel along all four sides for hemstitching.

3. Work a hemstitch using the sewing thread around each of the thread groups created by each square in the fabric. They are easy to see, and no counting is required. See page 76 for detailed instructions and illustration. After you have completed the hemstitching, remove the threads in the fabric beyond the hemstitching, creating a self-fringed edging.

4. If you'd like to work the open area in the center of the mat as shown on page 31, clip and remove the threads seven rows beyond the outside edge of the border, and work the hemstitch along both sides of the channel. This step is optional.

NAPKIN RING

Directions

1. To make the napkin ring, work the design on a scrap of Aida cloth using the same thread. Trim away the excess Aida to within seven squares of all four sides of the band. Cut a scrap of the red wool felt the same length as the band, but cut it 1" wider.

2. Lay the stitched band along one long edge of the felt, right sides facing. Stitch along the edge with a $1/4$-inch seam allowance. Next, align the remaining long edge with the opposite long edge of the felt and stitch in the same manner.

3. Turn the resulting tube right side out and center the embroidered area on the red felt, forming a self-edging along each long side. Tuck the ends of the tube to the inside by $1/4$ inch and bring the two short edges together. Using invisible hand stitches, stitch the short ends together to make a ring.

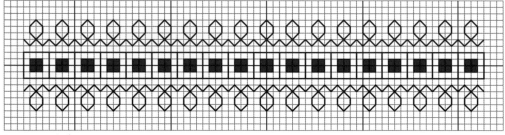

■ cross-stitch
╲ backstitch

Full-Size Pattern for Napkin Ring

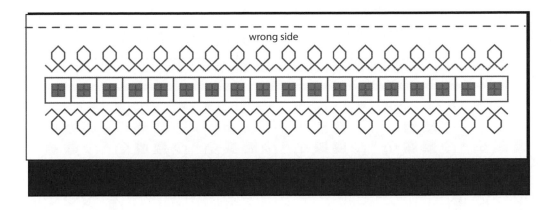

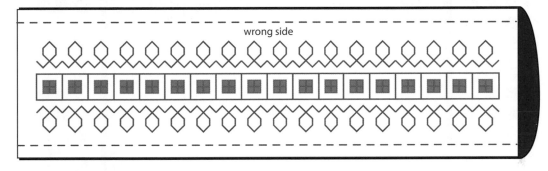

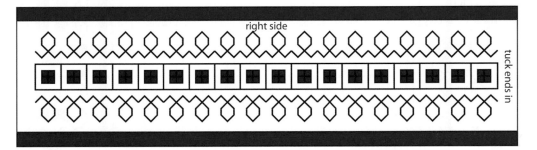

Stitching the Backing

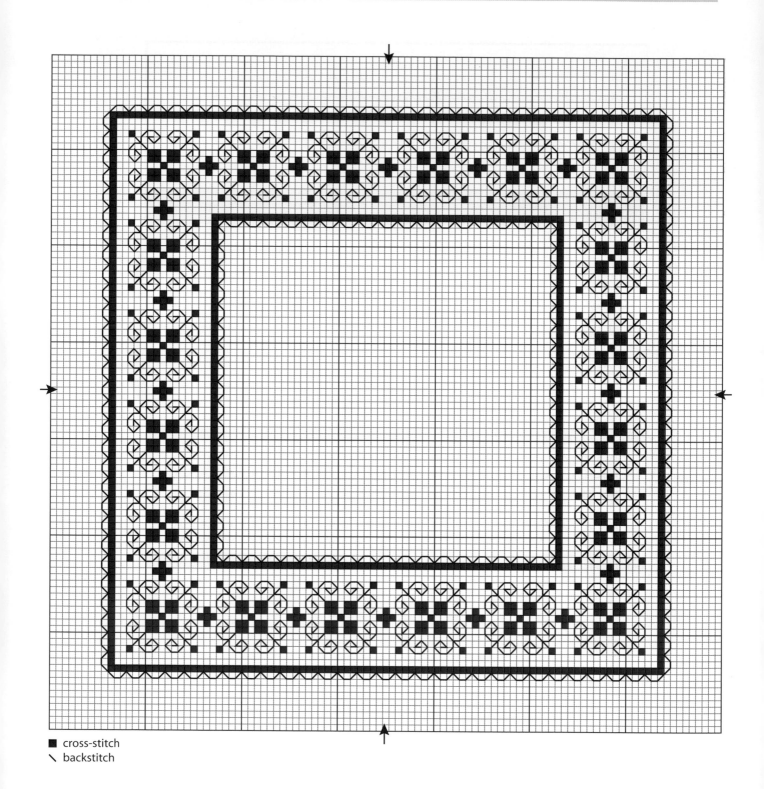

■ cross-stitch
\ backstitch

Full-Size Pattern for Candle Mat

Embroidered Ornaments and Wine Bag

Whether these motifs remind you of frosted holiday cookies, snowflakes, or northern European folk art, the designs are fun to stitch and can be used on any number of items. In these projects I have used the motifs—two different ones—to make a gift bag that's the perfect size for a bottle of wine, and some matching ornaments.

I've used unbleached, natural Osnaburg fabric to give the items an Old World look, but you can substitute white, off-white, or any other color of plainweave linen or cotton fabric instead. Even broadcloth can be used.

Materials Needed

- ▢ ¹/₂ yard unbleached Osnaburg fabric
- ▢ Water-soluble fabric marking pen
- ▢ Sewing thread to match fabric
- ▢ DMC 6-strand embroidery floss in colors 906 Medium Parrot Green, 996 Medium Electric Blue, B5200 Snow White, and 817 Very Dark Coral Red
- ▢ Size 9 embroidery needle
- ▢ Matching trim or ribbon for ornaments
- ▢ Scrap of grosgrain ribbon

ORNAMENTS

Directions

1. Trace the shapes onto the Osnaburg fabric, spacing the motifs at least 4 inches apart to leave enough space for seam allowances.
2. Using two strands of the 6-strand floss and the needle, embroider the motifs using backstitch, fern stitch, detached chain stitch, French knots, and lazy daisy. Use the four colors of floss differently in each ornament. There are endless possibilities for variety just by varying where each color is used on each ornament.
3. To finish the ornaments, refer to pages 74–75 for assembly instructions.

WINE BAG

Directions

1. From the Osnaburg fabric cut two rectangles $7^1/2$" x $15^1/2$". On one of the rectangles mark the motif of choice using a water-soluble marking pen or other marking method, spacing the bottom tip of the motif 6 inches from the bottom edge of the rectangle. Set aside the second rectangle to be used as the bag backing.
2. Using two strands of the 6-strand floss and the needle, embroider the motif on the bag front using backstitch, fern stitch, detached chain stitch, French knots, and lazy daisy. You can use the colors anywhere you'd like, or refer to the color photo of the bag to stitch using the same colors.
3. To assemble the bag, place the two rectangles of Osnaburg together, right sides facing. Using the sewing thread, machine stitch $1/4$ inch from the edges of the rectangles, leaving the top edge unstitched.
4. Clip the two bottom corners and press the seam allowances on the sides and bottom of the bag open. Fold the bottom of the bag so that the bottom seam aligns with each side edge of the bag. Stitch across the bottom of the bag $1^1/2$ inches from the corner to pleat the bag bottom.
5. Turn the bag right side out. Fold under $1/4$ inch twice toward the inside of the bag to make a double hem around the top edge of the bag. Stitch the narrow hem in place by machine. Insert the bottle and tie the bag closed with a piece of coordinating grosgrain ribbon.

Embroidery Design

Full-Size Patterns

6 inches from
the bottom edge

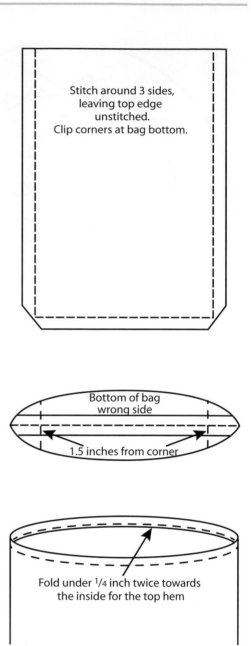

Stitch around 3 sides,
leaving top edge
unstitched.
Clip corners at bag bottom.

Bottom of bag
wrong side

1.5 inches from corner

Fold under 1/4 inch twice towards
the inside for the top hem

Bag Assembly

Naughty or Nice
Framed Hoop

A simple wooden embroidery hoop was used to frame this fun decoration. Hang it on the wall in the entry to remind everyone to be nice—or face the consequences. Nobody wants coal in their stocking!

Simple, easy stitches were used to make the project—and don't let the cuff filling of French knots deter you. They're easy to work once you get the hang of it, and making them repeatedly is terrific practice.

Materials Needed

- 16" x 16" piece of 32-count linen fabric in white or natural
- Water-soluble fabric marking pen
- DMC 6-strand embroidery floss in colors 666 Bright Red, B5200 Snow White, 470 Light Avocado Green, and 909 Very Dark Emerald Green
- Size 9 embroidery needle
- 8" wood embroidery hoop
- ½ yard of ¾" grosgrain ribbon in red
- Green craft paint to match the lighter green floss
- Paintbrush
- Craft glue

Directions

1. Trace the embroidery design onto the fabric using a water-soluble fabric marking pen, centering it on the fabric. Referring to the Color Key below, embroider the designs using two strands of the 6-strand embroidery floss in backstitch for the solid lines and French knots for the dotted lines and as a filling on the cuffs.

2. After completing the embroidery, wash the piece to remove the markings, let it dry, and press lightly. While the fabric is drying, separate the two rings of the embroidery hoop and paint each ring using the craft paint. Allow the paint to dry overnight.

3. After the paint has dried, center the completed embroidery in the hoop and tighten down the thumb screw, keeping the design perfectly centered by tugging the fabric edges as you tighten to move the fabric where needed.

4. Trim the excess fabric from the back side of the hoop to within ½ inch of the wood. Glue the edges of the fabric to the inside edge of the innermost hoop to secure it, being careful not to get any glue on the back side of the embroidered area.

5. Tie the ribbon into a 16-inch loop and attach the loop to the closure area of the hoop. Tie the tails into a bow to complete the project.

—— 666 red
—— 470 light green
—— 909 dark green

Color Key

Full-Size Pattern

Heartfelt Christmas Ornaments

These dainty little ornaments are in the shape of a heart, enhanced with swirling curlicues and pine boughs. Their small size makes them ideal as package toppers for loved ones or to hang on the knob of an antique cabinet as a decorative accent. Of course, you can always use them on the tree as well! The Noel Banner (pages 44–47) uses the same threads and fabrics, if you're wanting a matched set.

Materials Needed

- 12" x 16" piece of 32-count linen fabric in white or natural
- Water-soluble fabric marking pen
- DMC 6-strand embroidery floss in colors 498 Dark Red, 320 Medium Pistachio Green, and 612 Light Drab Brown
- Size 11/0 red glass seed beads, 18 per ornament
- Size 10 embroidery needle
- Beading needle
- Lightweight iron-on interfacing
- Scraps of green and red wool felt
- Scraps of red trim for the ornament edging

Directions

1. Trace the heart shape onto the fabric using a water-soluble fabric marking pen. Referring to the Color Key, embroider the designs using two strands of the 6-strand embroidery floss in backstitch for the tendrils and branches, and straight stitch for the pine needles.

2. Using the beading needle and matching thread, stitch on beads as indicated by the red dots.

3. After completing the embroidery and adding the beads, fuse a scrap of interfacing to the back side of each heart to give it some body, and finish as an ornament. Refer to the finishing instructions on pages 74–75.

Full-Size Pattern

— 498 red
— 320 green
— 612 light brown
● seed bead

Color Key

Noel Banner

Combine embroidered evenweave linen with colorful wool felt to make these sturdy ornaments that can be combined to make a pennant banner or used individually. Three colors of wired Memory Thread from DMC were used to make the cording holding the individual sections. The wire makes it easy to attach to almost anything without taping or nailing—simply twist the ends into hooks or loops and attach to door knobs, candlesticks on a fireplace, or around a simple wreath of fresh greenery.

Materials Needed

- 16" x 16" piece of 32-count linen fabric in white or natural
- Water-soluble fabric marking pen
- DMC 6-strand embroidery floss in colors 498 Dark Red, 320 Medium Pistachio Green, and 612 Light Drab Brown
- Size 11/0 red glass seed beads, 6 per letter
- Size 10 embroidery needle
- Beading needle
- Lightweight iron-on interfacing
- Scraps of green and red wool felt
- Scraps of narrow polka dot ribbon
- Machine sewing thread to match the fabric and the red felt
- DMC Memory Thread in white, red, and green

Directions

1. Trace the four individual shapes on the fabric using a water-soluble fabric marking pen. Referring to the Color Key on page 47, embroider the designs using two strands of the 6-strand embroidery floss in backstitch for the tendrils and lettering borders, straight stitch for the pine needles, and seed stitch inside the letters.

2. Using the beading needle and matching thread, stitch three beads to the upper tendril and three to the lower tendril.

3. Iron the interfacing to the back side of the fabric and cut out the individual shapes. Lay the shapes on the green felt, spacing them about an inch apart. Using the machine sewing thread that matches the fabric, stitch the shapes onto the felt using a narrow, open zigzag. Using pinking shears, cut out each ornament 1/4 inch from the stitching.

4. Repeat with the red felt, stitching directly over your first line of zigzag stitching. To give the shapes more body, lay a second piece of felt under the shapes and, using the red sewing thread, zigzag around the shape 1/2 inch from the edges of the green felt. Cut away the excess red felt using the pinking shears, just outside the zigzag stitching line.

5. Cut an 8-inch length of the polka dot ribbon for each ornament. Tie it into a bow and tack one bow to the top of each ornament.

6. To make the hanging cording (optional), cut a 40-inch length from each color of Memory Thread. Holding the ends of all three lengths in one hand, twist the Memory Thread with the other hand to make a three-color wired trim. Tack the ornaments to the trim to use as a pennant banner.

machine zigzag stitch

pinked edges

Assembly

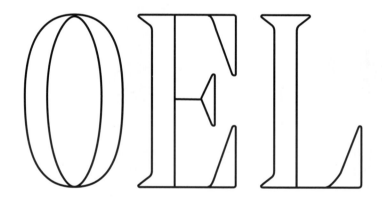

Full-Size Pattern

— 498 red
— 320 green
— 612 light brown
⊙ seed bead

Color Key

Christmas Star

This pretty Christmas Star was made as a tree topper. A length of ribbon or extra edge trim is attached at the back of the star, which allows it to be tied to the top of the tree. To make smaller versions of the star as ornaments, reduce the size of the pattern and use similar shades of 6-strand embroidery floss, embroidering the design in the same stitches, using just one or two strands of the floss (depending on how small you are making the ornaments). Or, enlarge the design, stitch using thicker thread, and use the star as an accent pillow on a chair near the fireplace.

Materials Needed

- Two 14" x 14" pieces of 40-count Newcastle Linen, white
- Water-soluble fabric marking pen
- Rainbow Gallery Elegance in colors E907 (green) and E820 (red)
- 14" x 14" piece of lightweight iron-on woven interfacing
- All-purpose sewing thread
- Polyester fiberfill

Directions

1. Edge-finish the two pieces of fabric. Fold one of the pieces of fabric into quarters to locate the center. Trace the star design on the fabric using a water-soluble fabric marking pen, centering the design on the fabric. Reserve the second piece for the backing.

2. Embroider the design referring to the Color Key. Using E820, embroider the red areas of the design. The curlicues are embroidered in backstitch, and the central star in lazy daisy. Using E907, embroider the small leaves in detached chain, the dots in French knots, and the dashed lines in running stitch.

3. After the embroidery has been completed, wash and press the stitched design. Trim any straggling tails on the back side of the piece.

4. Fuse the interfacing to the back side of the stitched design. Place the fused embroidered design and the reserved backing fabric together, with right sides facing. Using white all-purpose sewing thread, stitch around the star $1/4$ inch from the running stitch outlines. Leave a small opening along one side of a star leg for turning.

5. Clip the corners and turn the star right side out through the opening. Press and stuff lightly with fiberfill. Hand stitch the opening closed using the all-purpose thread.

6. Carefully hand stitch the trim to the edges of the star. Extra trim can be used to make a hanging loop, or use ribbon to make ties for attaching to the treetop.

━ E907 green
━ E820 red

Color Key

Full-Size Pattern

"We Wish You a Merry Christmas" Framed Sampler

This easy sampler can be stitched quickly using just two colors of floss in blue. If blue is not your choice for holiday colors, stitch it using two shades of red, two shades of green—or your own color choice. The design fits a standard 8" x 10" frame.

Materials Needed

- 16" x 18" piece of natural-colored plainweave broadcloth or other densely woven fabric
- Water-soluble fabric marking pen
- DMC 6-strand embroidery floss in colors 3808 Ultra Very Dark Turquoise and 3845 Medium Bright Turquoise
- Size 10 embroidery needle
- 8" x 10" inch frame of your choice
- Foam-core backer board

51

Directions

1. Transfer the design onto the fabric using a water-soluble fabric marking pen, centering the design on the fabric. If you have difficulty seeing the pattern through the fabric, use a light box, or trace the design by holding the fabric and pattern up to a window.

2. Embroider the design using two strands of the 6-strand embroidery floss throughout, following the Color Key. Solid lines are worked in stem stitch and the dashed lines in running stitch. Each snowflake is worked using straight stitch in the center, with fern stitch along the arms of the snowflakes.

3. When you have completed the embroidery and washed out the markings, mount the design on a piece of foam-core board cut to fit the inside area of the frame. Directions for mounting an embroidery can be found on pages 68–69.

—— 3808 dark turquoise
—— 3845 bright turquoise

Color Key

Full-Size Pattern

Felt Peppermints

Stitch up a batch of felt peppermint wheels and display them in a pretty bowl for the holidays. The materials listed are enough to produce about twelve to sixteen 3¹/₂-inch peppermints.

Materials Needed

- ▪ Two 12" x 18" pieces each of red, green, and white wool felt
- ▪ DMC Size 5 pearl cotton in B5200 Snow White, 904 Very Dark Parrot Green, 304 Medium Red, and 743 Medium Yellow
- ▪ Size 4 crewel needles
- ▪ Assorted buttons up to 1 inch wide in green and yellow
- ▪ Craft glue or felt glue
- ▪ All-purpose sewing thread in colors to match felt

Directions

1. Set aside one of each color of the felt pieces to use for the backings. Cut the pattern pieces from the remaining three pieces of felt, cutting the large circles first, followed by the small center circles and the spokes of the candy wheels.

2. Glue the felt pieces to the larger circles. Feel free to mix and match the colors of the thread and felt and be creative! Let the glue dry at least 24 hours.

3. Using the pearl cotton, embroider the details on each candy wheel front in backstitch, detached chain stitch, and/or French knots. Stitch through all layers (the glue is flexible enough to stitch through).

4. Stitch a button to the front center of each candy wheel.

5. Place the embroidered candy wheels face down on the remaining felt pieces, using felt that matches the large circles. Pin in place. Using all-purpose sewing thread, stitch around the edges of the circle, leaving a $^{1}/_{4}$-inch seam allowance and a $1^{1}/_{2}$-inch opening for turning.

6. Cut the circles from the backing using pinking shears. You can also use regular shears, but you will need to clip the edges of the seam allowances before turning. Turn each circle right side out and stuff lightly. Hand stitch the openings closed.

Embroidery Guide

Full-Size Patterns

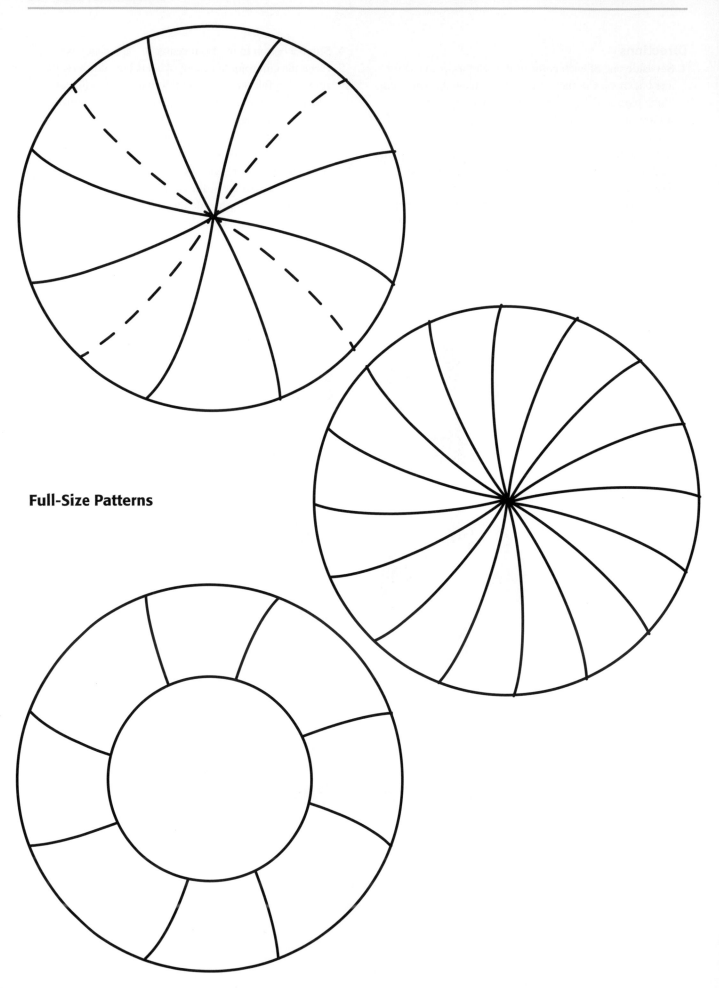

Stitch Guide

The following stitches are used in the projects in this book.

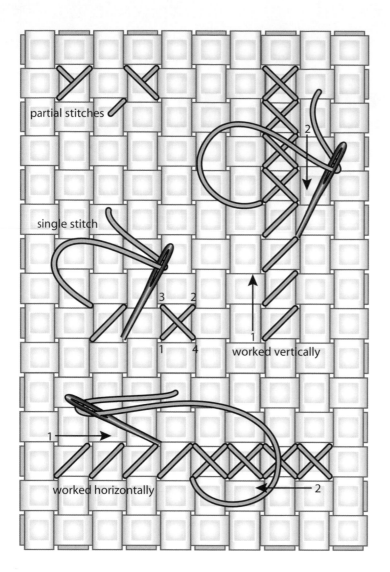

partial stitches

single stitch

worked vertically

worked horizontally

Cross-Stitch on Aida

Cross-stitch can be worked as a counted stitch over a single square on Aida fabric, or over two threads when using an evenweave fabric. It can also be used in a surface-embroidery project by carefully marking the surface of the fabric. Each stitch is comprised of two diagonal stitches that cross in the center. They can be worked individually as well as in vertical and horizontal rows. Keep the stitches uniform by making sure the top stitch always crosses in the same direction, from upper left to lower right. When working a counted chart, you may also find that partial stitches are used, usually a half or quarter stitch.

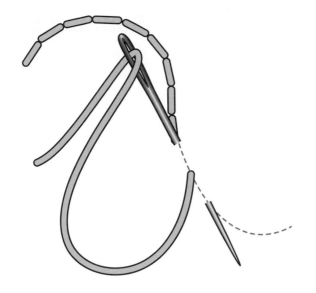

Backstitch

Backstitch is used to outline a shape, and is worked in a "two steps forward, one step back" type of motion. To work the stitch, bring the needle up through the fabric a stitch-length's distance from the starting point and insert the needle at the starting point—working the stitch backward. Bring the needle up again a stitch-length's distance from the first stitch and continue working in this manner to the end.

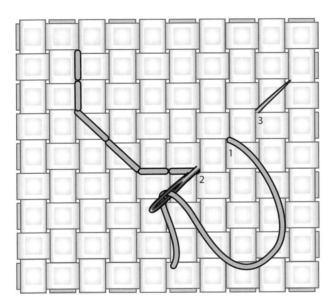

To work the stitch on Aida, work the stitches between the Aida squares, or diagonally across a square.

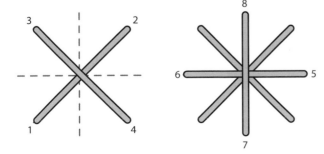

Double Cross-Stitch or Star Stitch

A double cross-stitch is comprised of a single, standard cross-stitch followed by an upright cross-stitch. This stitch can be used to make stars, fillings, and decorative borders or bands in a project.

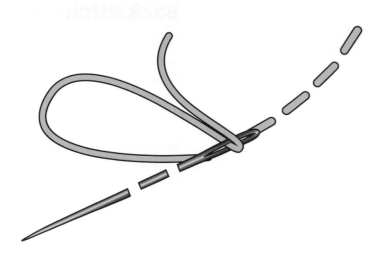

Running Stitch

Running stitch is worked using a basic—almost intuitive—in and out motion of the needle. This stitch is usually used to outline a shape. It can be worked in any length and spacing, but should be kept consistent throughout the area being stitched.

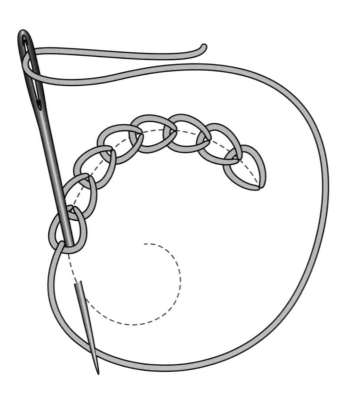

Chain Stitch

Standard chain stitch is worked along a marked line using small, looped stitches. It can be used to outline a shape or be worked in concentric circles or rows as a filling stitch.

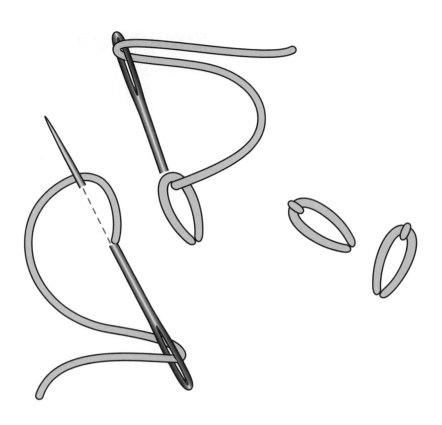

Detached Chain Stitch

Detached chain stitch is similar to chain stitch. However, instead of making a chain of multiple stitches, a single looped stitch is made, held in place with a small tacking stitch at the opposite end of the loop. Detached chain forms the basis of the lazy daisy stitch.

Lazy Daisy

A lazy daisy is a group of detached chain stitches worked around a center point to make a flower or small blossom.

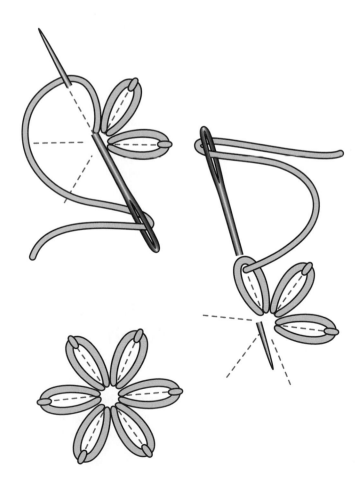

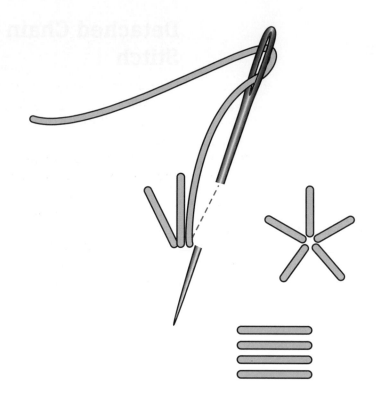

Straight Stitch

Straight stitch is just a single stitch, but can be used in different lengths and in groups to make other stitches or motifs. In these examples, straight stitches have been used to make a decorative, repeating element in a border; create a star; and line up horizontally.

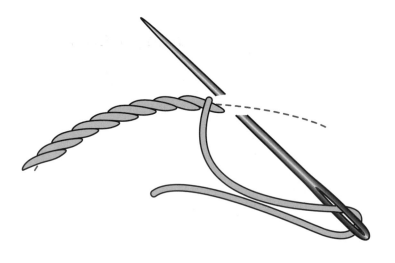

Stem Stitch

Stem stitch is a basic stitch that produces a solid line of stitching. This stitch can be used to outline shapes, or as stems and tendrils in a project. The stitch is worked by taking tiny stitches backward along the outline of the shape with the working thread held below the needle, and with each stitch slightly covering the previous stitch. Rows of closely spaced stem stitch can also be used as a filling stitch.

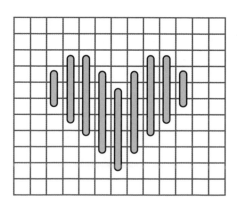

Counted Satin Stitch

Counted satin stitch is worked on evenweave fabric, with the stitches passing in between the fibers in the fabric. This stitch can be used to make individual motifs or geometric borders.

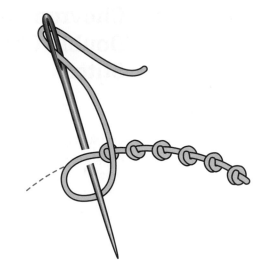

Coral Stitch

Coral stitch is worked by wrapping the thread around the needle while stitching, making small knots along the stitching line. It gives a textured effect that looks pretty worked as an outline.

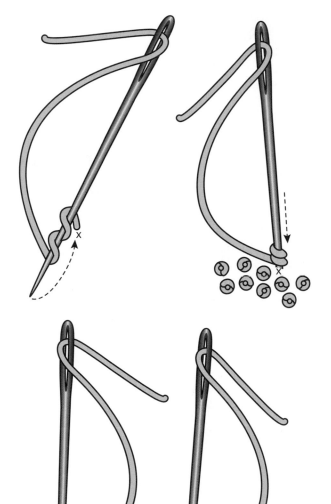

French Knots

French knots are easy to work once you've practiced them. To work a knot, bring the needle up through the fabric and wrap the working thread around the needle twice. Insert the needle back into the fabric very close to, but not in, the same hole as you came out of and pull the thread through, guiding the thread with your opposite hand as it passes through the fabric. Do not wrap too tightly, or you'll have a difficult time pulling the needle through the knot. The thread should be against the needle, but not snug or tight. If your knot pulls through to the other side when working the stitch, try loosening the wrap a bit, and make sure you're not going down into the same hole—you need a bridge to hold the knot on the surface (usually just a fiber or two in the fabric will suffice).

French knots with tails are made in the same way as a standard French knot, with the exception of inserting the needle into the fabric a short distance from the hole you originally came up in.

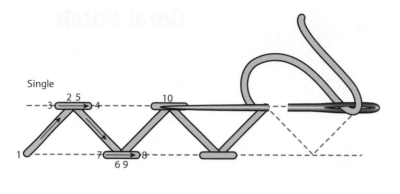

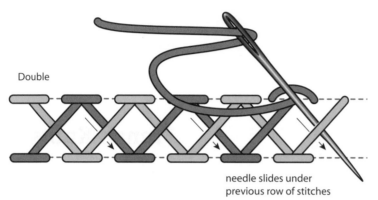

needle slides under
previous row of stitches

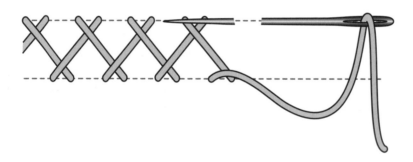

Chevron and Double Chevron Stitch

The chevron stitch is best used in rows and borders. It features a zigzagging stitch topped by a straight, horizontal stitch. It is easiest to work as a counted-thread stitch, but can also be used for surface embroidery by carefully marking the spacing on the fabric using a water-soluble fabric marking pen or pencil.

Herringbone Stitch

This decorative stitch forms overlapping zigzagging lines of stitching that are perfect for rows and borders or to outline a shape. It is easiest to work as a counted-thread stitch, but can also be worked in a surface-embroidery project by carefully spacing or premarking the stitches on the fabric. This stitch looks terrific with ribbon threaded through it.

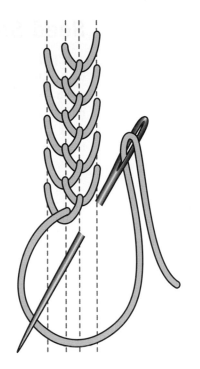

Feather Stitch

This versatile, textured stitch is a master of illusion. Worked closely spaced, the stitch makes a thicker border or band. Worked farther apart, the stitch is open, airy, and thin. Use this stitch in borders and rows or to outline shapes. It also mimics thorny stems and seaweed beautifully.

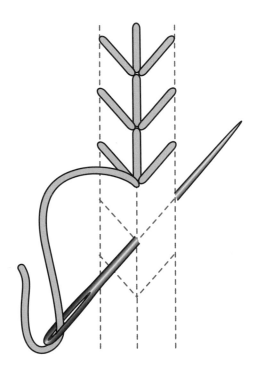

Fern Stitch

This easy, textured stitch is worked in three straight stitches, with the insertion point for each stitch at the base of each three-stitch group. These groups are worked repeatedly along the line of stitching. Be sure to space and work each group uniformly for best results.

Seed Stitch

This is a simple, dainty filling stitch, worked by making a small, straight stitch—much like a seed—at regular intervals. Work the stitches far apart for a light, airy filling or closer together for a denser filling.

Finishing Basics

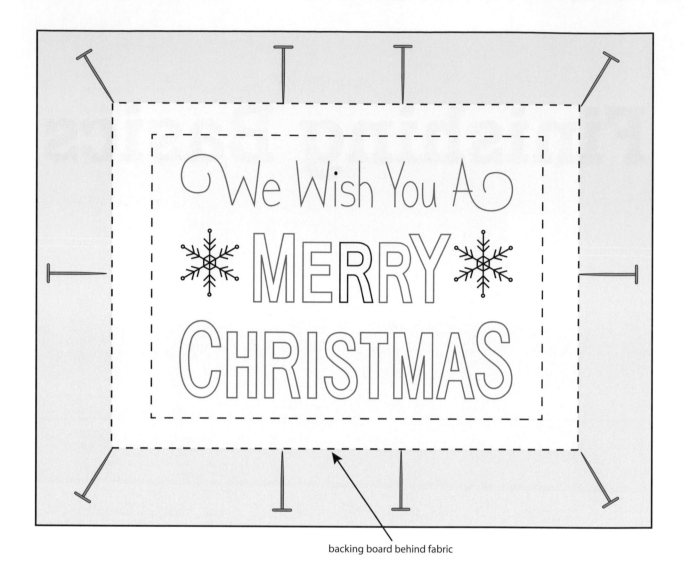

backing board behind fabric

Mounting for Framing

1. To frame a finished piece, cut a piece of acid-free foam-core board to fit the inside measurements of the frame you are using.
2. If desired, pad the board lightly by gluing on a piece of flat (low-loft) cotton batting using acid-free glue.
3. Center the embroidered piece over the board and hold it in position using T-pins along the sides and corners to prevent shifting.
4. Fold the excess fabric to the back side of the board and secure the piece using lacing stitches as shown. The stitching should be tight enough to hold the material in place, but should not stretch the fabric.
5. Remove the T-pins, insert the panel into the frame, and secure in place.

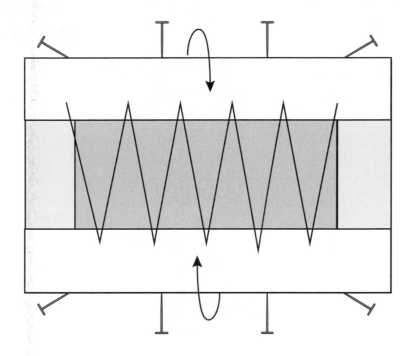

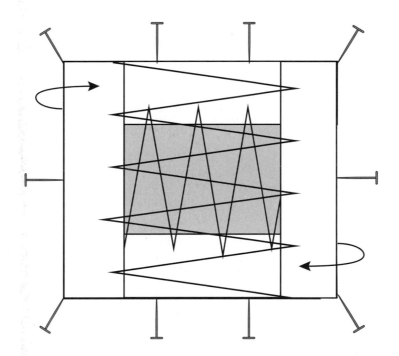

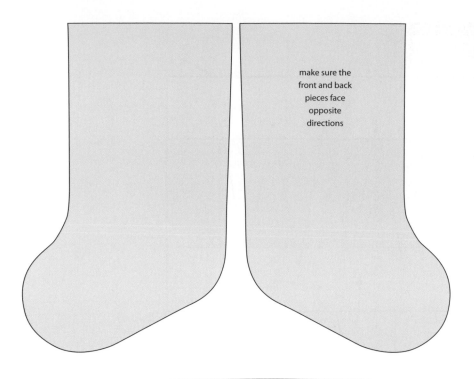

make sure the
front and back
pieces face
opposite
directions

Finishing a Stocking

1. To finish a stocking, trim down the stocking front to the cutting line. Use the stocking front as a pattern for cutting the back piece the exact same size (for one-sided fabrics, place them wrong sides together before cutting so you won't have two pieces each facing the same direction—they need to face in opposite directions).

2. Place the stocking front and back piece together, with their right sides facing. Stitch around the stocking using a $1/4$-inch seam allowance in matching thread. Leave the top opening unstitched.

3. Clip the curved edges around the toe and heel and turn the stocking right side out.

4. Cut a 1-inch binding strip for the top edge from matching or contrasting felt or fabric. Fold one short end under $1/4$ inch. Stitch the binding around the top edge, with the right side of the binding strip facing the right side of the stocking. Start at the side seam, and overlap the ends slightly when returning to the starting point.

5. Fold the binding to the inside of the stocking. Fold under a narrow hem and hand stitch the binding to the inside of the stocking.

6. To make a hanging loop, cut a matching piece of fabric 5" x $1^{1}/_{2}$". Fold the strip in half lengthwise, with right sides together. Stitch along the long edge using a $1/4$-inch seam allowance. Turn the resulting tube right side out, centering the seam along the strip. Fold the strip in half, seams together.

7. Hand stitch the hanging loop to the inside of the side edge of the stocking, hiding the ends inside the stocking.

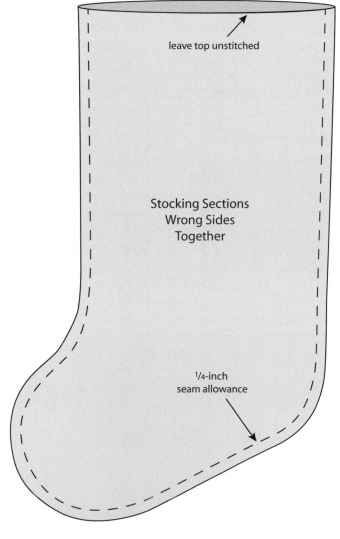

leave top unstitched

Stocking Sections
Wrong Sides
Together

$1/4$-inch
seam allowance

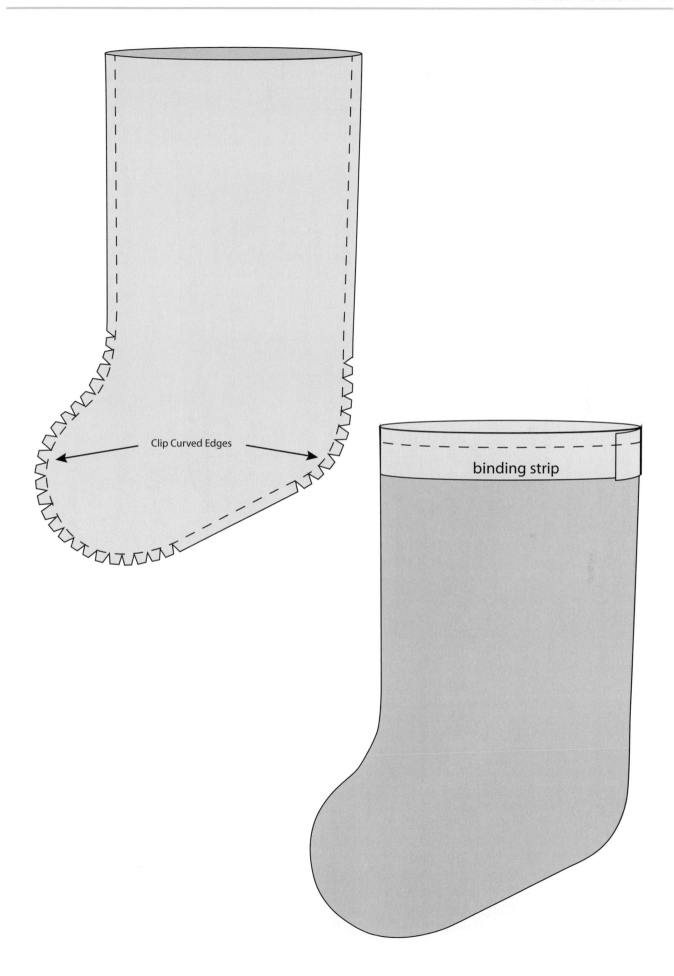

Clip Curved Edges

binding strip

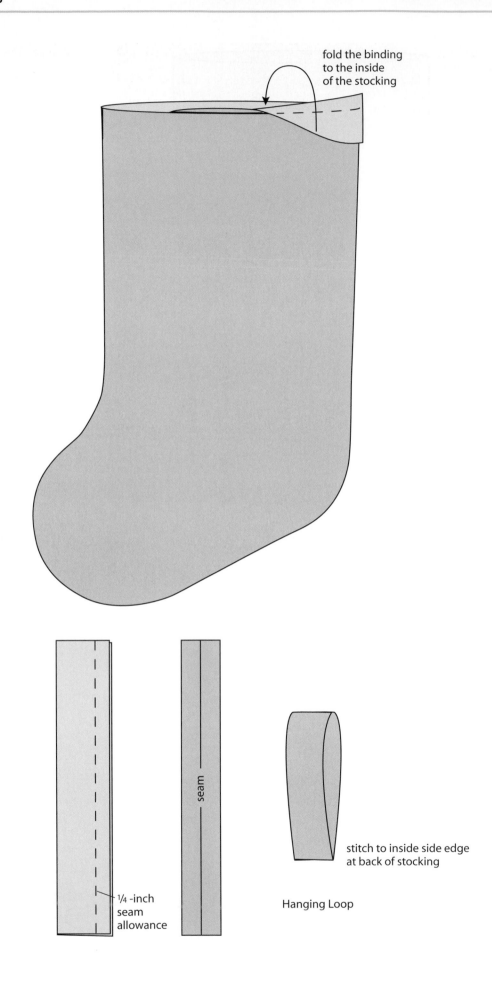

fold the binding
to the inside
of the stocking

¼-inch
seam
allowance

seam

stitch to inside side edge
at back of stocking

Hanging Loop

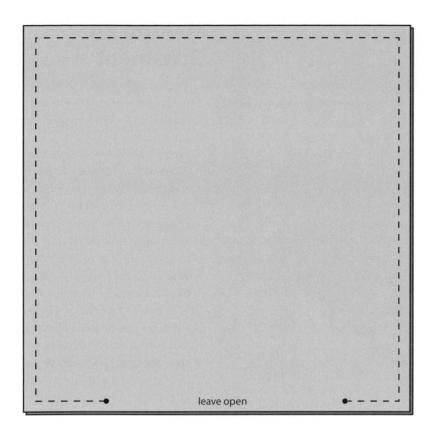

leave open

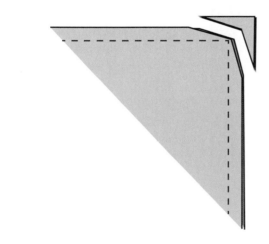

Making a Pillow Cover

1. Trim down the embroidered piece to within 1 inch of the desired size so that you will have a $1/2$-inch seam allowance on each side. If adding borders, cut the borders from fabric and stitch in place, right sides together, using matching sewing thread and a $1/2$-inch seam allowance. Press the borders outward and press to make a pillow top.

2. Cut a piece of backing fabric the same size as the pillow top. Stitch the backing and the pillow top together, right sides facing, using a $1/2$-inch seam allowance. Leave the bottom edge partially open for turning and stuffing.

3. Clip the corners close to—but not through—the stitching. Turn the pillow cover right side out through the opening at the bottom and insert a pillow form or stuff using fiberfill.

4. Hand stitch the bottom opening closed using matching sewing thread.

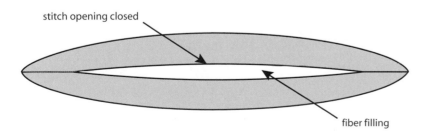

stitch opening closed

fiber filling

leave open

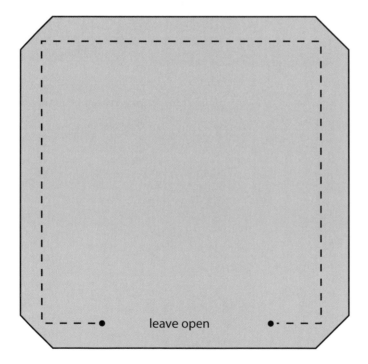

leave open

Making an Ornament

1. An ornament is made in the same manner as a pillow, but on a smaller scale. You can follow the same directions as given for Making a Pillow Cover on page 73. However, if the ornament is round, clip the outsides edges after stitching to reduce bulk in the seam allowances.

2. To attach a cord trim with a hanging loop, cut a length of trim about 8 inches longer than the circumference of the outside edge of the stuffed ornament. Open a small hole in the seam allowance at the top center of the ornament (just one or two slipped stitches should suffice) and insert $^1/_2$ inch of one end of the trim into the hole.

3. Using sewing thread to match the trim, hand stitch the trim around the outside edges of the ornament. The trim will cover the seam line.

4. When you reach the starting point, cut away the excess trim leaving a 5- to 7-inch tail. Form a loop with the tail and insert $^1/_2$ inch of the end into the same hole as the starting end. Secure the ends in place with a few invisible stitches and close the hole.

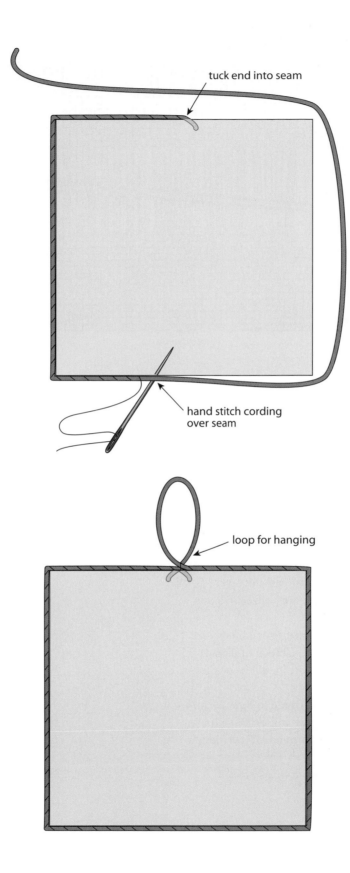

tuck end into seam

hand stitch cording
over seam

loop for hanging

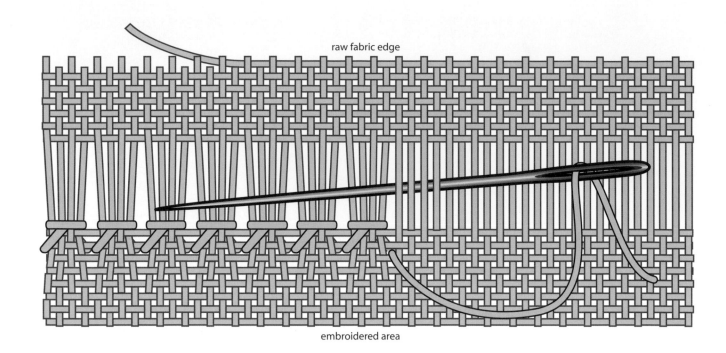

raw fabric edge

embroidered area

Fringing Fabric Edges

Making a fringed edge is a pretty way to finish small items like coasters or doilies and is actually very easy to do. This type of edge can be worked on nearly any evenweave fabric or Aida fabric. To work the fringe:

1. Decide how far from the stitched edge you want the fringe to be. For example, if you want the fringe $^1/_2$ inch from the edges, count the number of threads that are in the $^1/_2$-inch space along all four sides.
2. Next, remove one or two threads just past the measurement in step 1, creating an open space. Do this along all four sides.
3. Work the basic hemstitch in the space, around four threads on an evenweave fabric and a block of threads on Aida fabric. The anchoring thread should be on the embroidery side of the open space.
4. Determine how long you want the fringe to be and trim the fabric. For example, if the fringe will be $^3/_4$-inch wide, trim away the excess fabric around all four sides $^3/_4$ inch from the hemstitching.
5. Remove the fibers from the fabric along all sides to create the fringe.

Recommended Resources

Every stitcher has favorite web sites featuring inspiration, tutorials, or supplies. These are a few of my favorites.

Educational Sites

NeedleKnowledge
http://needleknowledge.com
This site is a terrific resource for embroidery enthusiasts and features free patterns, stitch tutorials, links to educational videos, and other material useful to stitchers.

DMC's *Emma Broidery* Blog:
http://dmc-threads.com
This blog, offered by DMC USA, features news and information about what's new on the needlework scene, as well as free patterns and projects for all stitching levels, and is updated several times per week.

DMC USA
http://www.dmc-usa.com
Free patterns and projects can be found in the separate stitching categories, but the mother lode of freebies is located in the DMC Club area. It's free—just sign up and sign in at http://www.dmc-usa.com/DMC-Club.aspx

Mary Corbet's Needle 'N Thread
http://www.needlenthread.com
This site run by Mary Corbet features an extensive collection of stitch videos, book and pattern reviews, tips and advice, free patterns, and resources for stitchers. Be sure to sign up for her free newsletter.

Sharon B's Pin Tangle
http://pintangle.com
An excellent blog covering all things embroidery.

Royal School of Needlework
http://www.royal-needlework.org.uk
This UK-based group offers degree programs in the needlearts including hand embroidery courses for all levels; conservation, restoration, and repair of antique embroideries; and an extensive collection of needlework.

Guilds, Clubs, and Groups

The Embroiderers' Guild of America (EGA)
https://www.egausa.org
Established in 1958, the EGA offers members the opportunity to learn a wide variety of techniques, and offers professional certification through online and correspondence courses and national seminars.

The Embroiderers' Association of Canada (EAC)
http://www.eac.ca
This Canada-based nonprofit educational organization offers fellowship to people who enjoy needlework and wish to learn and share their knowledge. It offers classes and networking aimed at preserving and promoting traditional techniques.

National Academy of Needlearts (NAN)
http://www.needleart.org
Established in 1985, NAN has devoted itself to the advancement of embroidery as an art form and provides education to those interested in furthering their embroidery skills as teachers, judges, artists, designers, authors, and technically proficient embroiderers.

Embroiderers' Guild
http://www.embroiderersguild.com
This UK-based organization is known as an international voice for embroidery and offers members centralized and regional events, workshops, seminars, and exhibitions of fine historic and modern needlework. Its goal is to build awareness of stitch and textile art and offer inspiration to stitchers of all levels.

The Embroiderers' Guild of Queensland
http://www.embroiderersguildqld.org.au
This Australian guild's goal is to keep traditional forms of embroidery alive and to embrace new forms of stitching. It offers a wide range of classes for adults and children, which have been developed for skill levels from the beginner through to the accomplished embroiderer.

Suppliers

If you don't have a needlework retailer in your area or if they don't stock the needed items, here are several suggestions for online retailers. This list is by no means complete, but they are companies that I have used and trust. A quick search using the keywords "Embroidery materials and supplies" will yield an almost endless supply of options as well.

DMC USA
http://www.shopdmc.com

Herrschner's
http://www.herrschners.com

Yarn Tree
http://yarntree.com

Nordic Needle
http://www.nordicneedle.com

ABC Stitch
http://www.abcstitch.com

Terminology

Aida. A sturdy cotton fabric used for cross-stitch that has an open weave with a mesh of squares. A single cross-stitch is worked over each mesh square.

Beading needle. A long, thin needle with a small eye. It must be able to pass through the hole in a bead to attach it to the fabric.

Conversion chart. A chart that shows you the color numbers for the closest substitute for threads produced by different manufacturers (see pages 80–81).

Counted thread. The process of working a stitch over a designated number of warp and weft threads in the fabric, usually following a charted pattern. The pattern is not premarked on the surface.

Crocking. Dye transference resulting from washing or handling an embroidered piece.

Edge finishing. Securing the raw edges of fabric to avoid fraying as you work. It can included hemming or overstitching with either a zigzag sewing machine stitch or a serger.

Embroidery. Decorative stitching in thread, floss, or yarn on a fabric ground.

Embroidery needle. A sharp needle with a large eye. It is used when the needle must pierce the fabric rather than pass between the fibers in the fabric.

Embroidery scissors. Small scissors with sharp, pointed blades. The cutting blade is usually less than 2 inches. The smaller size makes them easy to tote in a work bag when stitching on the go.

Evenweave. Fabric with an identical number of warp and weft threads per inch. The individual threads in the fabric are easy to count and are used in counted-thread embroidery.

Felt. A heavy, non-woven fabric made of wool, acrylic, or a blend.

Floss. A common embroidery yarn, featuring six individual strands of thread that are separated before using.

Hank. Embroidery thread purchased in a looped and twisted bundle. Hanks are not the same as pull-skeins, and thread must be unwound for use. Pulling thread from a hank will result in tangling.

Over-dyed floss. Floss that has been dyed with multiple colors that blend where the colors overlap.

Plainweave. Fabric with an identical number of warp and weft threads per inch. The individual threads in the fabric are tightly woven and difficult to count, making this a good fabric for surface-embroidery projects. Fabrics may be produced from cotton, linen, hemp, or other natural fibers.

Self-fringe. A method of securing the threads in an evenweave or Aida fabric with hemstitching so that fibers in the fabric can be removed to make a fringe. The hemstitching holds the remaining fabric fibers in place and prevents fraying.

Skein. Embroidery thread in an easy-to-use bundle. The bundle is arranged so that the thread can be pulled from the skein to any desired length.

Stranded floss. Thread that is put up on a pull-skein in groups that can be separated, as in 6-strand embroidery floss.

Surface embroidery. Embroidery where the design is premarked on the surface of the fabric and worked in stitches that rest on top of the fabric.

Tapestry needle. A needle with an elongated eye and a blunt tip. Used when the needle must pass between the fibers in the fabric rather than through them.

Thread count. The number of warp and weft threads per square inch of fabric. The higher the thread count, the tighter the weave.

T-pins. Larger pins with a sharp point at one end and a folded, T-shaped end at the other. These pins are easy to grab and hold, and are used to anchor the fabric of completed projects to backings or blocking boards.

Variegated floss. Floss that contains more than one shade of a particular color family, with evenly spaced color gradations.

Warp. Lengthwise threads in a plainweave or evenweave fabric.

Water-soluble. A product that can be dissolved in water or can be washed from the fabric.

Weft. Crosswise threads in a plainweave or evenweave fabric.

Color Conversion and Metric Equivalent Charts

Color Conversion Chart

DMC thread numbers and names have been used in the projects in this book. If these threads are not available in your area, use the chart below to select the same colors from other brand names. The colors may vary slightly among manufacturers; the table below shows the closest available match.

DMC Color	DMC	Anchor	Sullivans
Variegated Red	115	1206	*
Medium Red	304	1006	45050
Medium Pistachio Green	320	215	45061
Light Avocado Green	470	267	45105
Dark Red	498	1005	45108
Light Drab Brown	612	832	45145
Bright Red	666	46	45155
Medium Yellow	743	302	45184
Very Dark Coral Red	817	13	45219
Very Dark Parrot Green	904	258	45253
Medium Parrot Green	906	256	45255
Very Dark Emerald Green	909	923	45257
Medium Electric Blue	996	433	45315
Ultra Very Dark Turquoise	3808	1068	45405
Medium Bright Turquoise	3845	1089	45443
Snow White	B5200	1	45002

* No equivalent match

Metric Equivalent Chart

1 inch = 2.54 centimeters

1 foot = 12 inches, 30.48 centimeters, or .30 meters

1 yard = 36 inches, 91.44 centimeters, or .91 meters

Index of Stitches

Backstitch 59
Chain Stitch 60
Chevron Stitch 64
Coral Stitch 63
Cross-Stitch 58
Detached Chain Stitch 61
Double Chevron Stitch 64
Double Cross-Stitch 59
Feather Stitch 65
Fern Stitch 65
French Knots 63
Herringbone Stitch 64
Lazy Daisy 61
Running Stitch 60
Satin Stitch 62
Seed Stitch 66
Star Stitch 59
Stem Stitch 62
Straight Stitch 62

Visual Index

Felt Stockings
12

Scandinavian Banded Stocking
22

Embroidered Nativity Figures
18

Banded Tree Centerpieces
26

Banded Candle Mat
and Napkin Ring **31**

Naughty or Nice Framed Hoop
39

Embroidered Ornaments and Wine Bag
35

Heartfelt Christmas Ornaments
42

Noel Banner
44

"We Wish You a Merry Christmas"
Framed Sampler   **51**

Christmas Star
48

Felt Peppermints
54

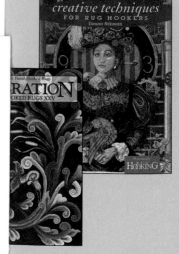